MW01244999

GRAMMAR'S SLAMMIN'
Punk-tuation Celebration

By: Pamela Hall
Illustrated by: Gary Currant

visit us at www.abdopublishing.com

Published by Magic Wagon, a division of the ABDO Group, 8000 West 78th Street, Edina, Minnesota 55439. Copyright © 2009 by Abdo Consulting Group, Inc. International copyrights reserved in all countries. All rights reserved. No part of this book may be reproduced in any form without written permission from the publisher.

Looking Glass Library™ is a trademark and logo of Magic Wagon.

Printed in the United States.

Text by Pamela Hall
Illustrations by Gary Currant
Edited by Stephanie Hedlund and Rochelle Baltzer
Interior layout and design by Neil Klinepier
Cover design by Neil Klinepier

Library of Congress Cataloging-in-Publication Data
Hall, Pamela.
  Punk-tuation celebration / by Pamela Hall ; illustrated by Gary Currant.
     p. cm. -- (Grammar's slammin')
  Includes bibliographical references.
  ISBN 978-1-60270-617-0
  1. English language--Punctuation--Juvenile literature. I. Currant, Gary, ill. II. Title.
  PE1450.H274 2009
  428.2--dc22
                               2008036327

"Yo!" cried Exclamation Point. "Let's have a bash!" Exclamation Point was always jazzed up about something.

"What if the place gets trashed?" asked Question Mark. "Won't we get in trouble?"
Question Mark questioned everything.

Period piped up, "Not to worry. Exclamation Point got the okay. It's cool." Period never got worked up. He just stated the facts.

"Let's make a list," suggested Comma. "We'll need tunes, balloons, food, and juice."

"Hey," interrupted Colon, "I rock at lists, too. Let's invite: all the punctuation marks."

Per

Dash –

'trophe

Hyphen -

Slash /

Hyphen came ready to rock. "I brought munchies," he said. "One-half are chips and one-half are peanuts."

Period thought Quotation Marks should run the karaoke. After all, they put marks around what everyone says.

"Yeah," yawned Apostrophe. "But I save time by combining two words into one."

Dash rushed up. "Excuse me—don't you see—you need me to add your extra comments."

"But you can't sort things out without me," said Apostrophe to slash. "Aren't those Hyphen's chips you're eating?"

17

"Whoa! Slow down!" cried Exclamation Point. "Don't get in a jumble! Let's get this Punk-tuation Celebration started!"

He jammed on the music and all the
punctuation marks started to dance.

Question Mark still had doubts. "Dude, what if we run out of food?"
"Everything's cool," Period said.

"That's good," sighed Comma,
"because look who just walked
through. So much for not running out
of food."

"Who invited them?" Question Mark asked.
"Hey, you're Nothing without us," claimed N.

25

The letters and punctuation marks rumbled together into a jumble of dots, dashes, and slashes . . .

Finally, Period picked himself up. "N's right. We need letters for words to punctuate. And they need punctuation to keep their meaning in line."

Exclamation Point agreed.
"Let's all get along and get
this party back on!"
And as far as we know,
they are still rockin' strong.

A Quick Guide to Punctuation

Apostrophe ' An apostrophe is used in contractions. These words show that some letters are missing. For example, when *was not* joins together, an apostrophe is added in place of the *o* to make *wasn't*. The apostrophe also pulls people and things together to show who owns something, as in: *Molly has a dog, so it is Molly's dog.*

Colon : A colon says, "Hey, pay attention! Here comes a list." It can also present an explanation for something. Or it can even introduce an important speech like: *She said: "My cat gives me: love, hugs, licks, and purrs."*

Comma , A comma says, "Slow down, pause, take a breath." It's great for separating things in a list, as in: *Alex likes pepperoni, black olives, and extra cheese on his pizza.*

Dash — The dash shows that some thought or idea is breaking up the sentence. If you throw the idea out, the sentence still makes sense. For example: *Jenny slept soundly—even with the tunes blasting—until the phone rang.*

Exclamation Point ! An exclamation point is used to really make a point. For example: *Bobby was tired of being treated like a baby!*

Hyphen - A hyphen is much shorter than a dash. It is used to pull some words together to make something new, such as: *a lemon-lime tree or one-third.* A hyphen can also be put at the end of a line to hold two parts of a word together.

Period . A period is used to state facts or to end a thought, as in: *The train will stop here. Or there.* Periods are also used in abbreviations. For example: *The party started at 7 a.m.*

Question Mark ? A question mark belongs at the end of a question. So: *Can you come to my party?*

Quotation Marks " These punctuation marks show that someone is talking. *"I don't want to use quotation marks," she said. But I told her, "If you don't, I won't know you are talking!"*

Slash / A slash gives you quick choices. It means or. *I can come today/tomorrow/next Thursday and I can bring my dog/cat/chicken.*

Web Sites

To learn more about grammar, visit ABDO Group online at www.abdopublishing.com. Web sites about grammar are featured on our Book Links page. These links are routinely monitored and updated to provide the most current information available.